What Do We Need at the Beach?

Seed Learning

sunscreen

swimsuit

towel

bucket

shovel

camera

goggles

sunglasses

What do we need at the beach?

We need sunscreen.

What do we need at the beach?

We need
a swimsuit.

What do we need at the beach?

We need a towel.

Let's learn more about Vietnam.

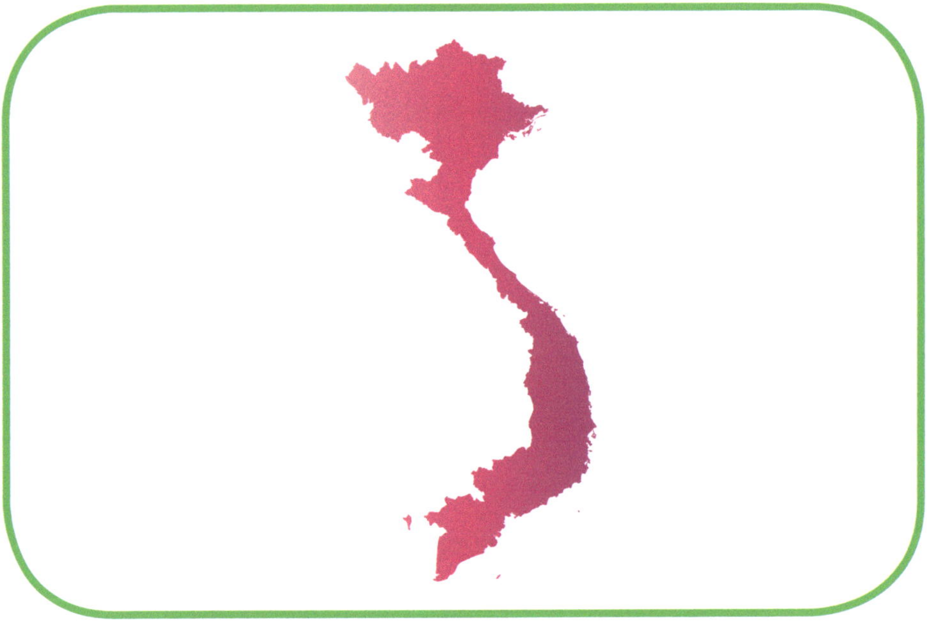

Bahn mi sandwich